UNDERSTANDING COMMON FIGURES OF SPEECH IN ENGLISH

For Students and Teachers of
English Studies

Table of Contents

CHAPTER ONE

What Are Figures of Speech?

Every day, we say things or hear people say things that mean something deeper than the words they use. Some of these expressions sound funny but their meanings don't get off your mind that easily. How could someone be a lion or look like a tiger? How could "bucket" replace the word "death?" These words are figures of speech and people use them sometimes.

Figures of speech are words, phrases and sentences that

have deeper meanings. Their meanings are often bigger and wider than the words themselves.

For instance, someone calls another person a fox. Does it mean that the other person is a real fox? No, the other person is a human being, not a wild animal. So why was he called a fox? It is because that person acts or behaves like a fox. A fox is cunning and, perhaps, that other person is cunning as well.

In this book, you will come across many figures of speech. It is important that you study them carefully and thoroughly. They are easy to learn and master.

CHAPTER TWO

Simile

Simile is a figure of speech that compares two objects. These two objects must be of different nature or different materials. For example, comparing a human being with another human is not simile. This is because humans have the same nature. But when you compare human beings with animals, you have achieved simile.

Simile makes its comparisons by using 'as' or 'like'. It states that something is like some other thing or that one thing is as the other one.

Another thing to keep in mind is that when using simile, you are merely saying that the two things you are comparing have similar quality or behavior.

Examples of Simile

1. He is like a lion.
2. She is like a dove.
3. We are like chickens.
4. Mary is like a tiger.
5. Sandra is like an angel.
6. Jack is like a fox.
7. My mother is as gentle as a dove.
8. His sister is as beautiful as an angel.

9. Her friend is as fierce as a lion.
10. Jake is as slow as a tortoise.
11. My back is as stiff as a board
12. The courtroom was as hot as hell.
13. Mom's words were as smooth as silk.
14. After her parents died, the house was as silent as the grave.
15. The kids are now as free as a bird.

Look at the examples again and notice how the two things compared together have different nature. It is no simile to say:

My sister is as beautiful as Queen Elizabeth.

'My sister' and 'Queen Elizabeth' are of the same nature. Both are human beings and the sentence does not qualify for simile.

More examples of Simile

1. He ran out of the room like an arrow shot from a bow.
2. She stood up tall like a cedar tree.
3. The answer is as clear as crystal.
4. Her memory is as unreliable as smoke.
5. Life is like a long story.
6. Love is like a butterfly.

7. Those insects were as dead as a doornail.
8. She wandered away from home like a lost cloud.
9. His problems became as bad as a sore.
10. Seeing you is like a dream come true.

Simile Using 'As'

1. The mayor is as proud as a peacock.
2. My friend is as slow as a sloth.
3. Right now we are as busy as a bee.
4. The accused is as innocent as a lamb.
5. My grandfather is as old as the hills.
6. The experience we had last night was as sweet as sugar.

7. The car moved as fast as a cheetah.
8. The old man is as blind as a bat.
9. The light bulb glowed as bright as the moon.
10. Peggy is as gentle as a lamb.
11. Her words are as sharp as a razor.
12. His body was as thin as a rake.
13. His advice is often as deep as the ocean.
14. We are now as bold as brass.
15. Since the accident, Mary became as cold as ice.
16. When she saw the movie, she became as white as a ghost.
17. His life is as clean as a whistle.

18.   Ted is as cunning as a fox.
19. My dad is as tough as leather.
20.   Her character is as good as gold.
21. My friend is as tall as a giraffe.

Simile Using 'Like'

1. Our coach made us to jump like a frog.
2. She climbs trees like a monkey.
3. Life is truly like a box of chocolate.
4. The injured dog slept like a baby.
5. The young fisherman swims like a fish.
6. The fat politician eats like a frog.

7. My two brothers always fight like cats and dogs.
8. My beautiful mom sings like a cuckoo.
9. I have eyes like a hawk.
10. The crowd chatters like a monkey.

Why We Use Simile

When you make a comparison between two things, you help others to clearly visualize what you mean. It works better when you use what people already know. For instance, the hills or mountains have existed before humans did. When you say someone is 'as old as the hills,' it helps readers and listeners to visualize how old the person is.

Once readers see the similarities between the two things, they understand you better. Use similes when you need to use them. They make your words and sentences richer and more attractive.

CHAPTER THREE

Metaphor

Remember that we use figures of speech to help people's mind to clearly see and understand what you say and mean. Good communication happens when readers and listeners can relate to what you're saying. If no one understands you, it means communication has failed.

Metaphor is similar to simile in a way. Unlike simile, a metaphor states that something is something else. A metaphor does not use 'like' or 'as' when making comparisons.

For example, when stating something as another, a metaphor says this thing is that thing. This is what makes it different from simile. Let's place simile and metaphor side by side to explain what we mean:

Simile: She is like an angel.

Metaphor: She is an angel.

Simile: He is like a pig.

Metaphor: He is a pig.

Simile: He is like a lion on the battlefield.

Metaphor: He is a lion on the battlefield.

Do you see how metaphors are similar to similes? The only difference is the omission of 'as' and 'like.'

Examples of Simple Metaphors

1. My neighbor is a couch potato.
2. The examination was a battlefield.
3. Her eyes are stars.
4. Our athletes were cheetahs in the race.
5. Alfred is a night owl.
6. Martha has a stone heart.
7. Danny is a firecracker.

8. His sister's eyes are diamonds.
9. We are shining stars.
10. My brother is an early bird.
11. My room is a prison.

Changing Similes to Metaphors

Simile: She is like a dove.

Metaphor: She is a dove.

Simile: We are like chickens.

Metaphor: We are chickens.

Simile: Mary is like a tiger.

Metaphor: Mary is a tiger.

Simile: Sandra is like an angel.

Metaphor: Sandra is an angel.

Simile: Jack is like a fox.

Metaphor: Jack is a fox.

Simile: My mother is as gentle as a dove.

Metaphor: My mother is a gentle dove.

Simile: His sister is as beautiful as an angel.

Metaphor: His sister is a beautiful angel.

Simile: Her friend is as fierce as a lion.

Metaphor: His friend is a fierce lion.

Simile: Jake is as slow as a tortoise.

Metaphor: Jake is a slow tortoise.

Simile: The mayor is as proud as a peacock.

Metaphor: The mayor is a peacock.

Simile: My friend is as slow as a sloth.

Metaphor: My friend is a sloth.

Simile: Right now we are as busy as a bee.

Metaphor: Right now we are busy bees.

Simile: The accused is as innocent as a lamb.

Metaphor: The accused is an innocent lamb.

Simile: My grandfather is as old as the hills.

Metaphor: My grandfather is the old hills.

Simile: The experience we had last night was as sweet as sugar.

Metaphor: The experience we had last night was sweet sugar.

Simile: The car is as fast as a cheetah.

Metaphor: The car is a cheetah.

Simile: The old man is as blind as a bat.

Metaphor: The old man is a blind bat.

Simile: The light bulb glowed as bright as the moon.

Metaphor: The light bulb is the moon.

Simile: Peggy is as gentle as a lamb.

Metaphor: Peggy is a lamb.

Simile: Her words are as sharp as a razor.

Metaphor: Her words are sharp razors.

Simile: His body was as thin as a rake.

Metaphor: His body is a thin rake.

Simile: His advice is as deep as the ocean.

Metaphor: His advice is a deep ocean.

Simile: We are now as bold as brass.

Metaphor: We are bold brass.

Simile: Since the accident, Mary became as cold as ice.

Metaphor: Since the accident, Mary is cold ice.

Simile: When she saw the movie, she became as white as a ghost.

Metaphor: When she saw the movie, she became a ghost.

Simile: His life is as clean as a whistle.

Metaphor: His life is a clean whistle.

Simile: Ted is as cunning as a fox.

Metaphor: Ted is a fox.

Simile: My dad is as tough as leather.

Metaphor: My dad is tough leather.

Simile: Her character is as good as gold.

Metaphor: Her character is gold.

Simile: My friend is as tall as a giraffe.

Metaphor: He is a giraffe.

Simile: Life is truly like a box of chocolate.

Metaphor: Life is a box of chocolate.

CHAPTER FOUR

Oxymoron

Have you ever had an experience that was both good and bad or bitter and sweet at the same time? How did you express it in a sentence? Did you say 'I had a bitter and sweet experience' or 'I had a bitter sweet experience'?

The second sentence is what oxymoron looks like. Oxymoron is a device or a speech technique that places two opposite words side by side. As in our example, bitter and sweet are placed close to each other. The two words must be opposites or they may not make a good example of oxymoron.

Examples of Oxymoron

1. This situation is **pretty ugly**.
2. Get me an **original copy** of that book.
3. We created a **virtual reality** for our company.
4. There was a **deafening silence** after the president made an announcement.
5. He's a **seriously funny** guy.
6. I think Jim is **growing smaller**.
7. The two boys had a **friendly fight**.

8. The witness said the **false truth**.
9. Our new plan is an **open secret**.
10. The **sweet sorrow** of graduating from school haunts everyone.

More Examples

1. A **small crowd** gathers here at nights.
2. The **cruel kindness** of my parents helped me grow up.
3. This movie is based on **true fiction**.
4. I was disappointed by her **foolish wisdom**.
5. The two friends walked **alone together**.
6. The police forced him to **climb down** the building.

7. Her **absent presence** made her popular in school.
8. The **civil war** lasted years.
9. The audience **clearly misunderstood** what he said.
10. He looked at her with **cool passion**.

More Examples

1. My **eloquent silence** bothers them so much.
2. What the mayor said is **falsely true**.
3. Tim's actions are **deceptively honest**.
4. The dog was **found missing**.
5. My uncle is a **guest host**.
6. Mr. Sam is now a **living dead**.

7. There was a **loud whisper** across the room.
8. She gave us **old news**.
9. She gave me a **sad smile** when I apologized.
10. We couldn't break the **soft rock**.
11. Jake is **terribly good** at mathematics.
12. Miss Adela is a **student teacher**.

CHAPTER FIVE

Personification

When you say that your TV is shouting, you're making it seem as though your TV is a living thing. When you say your door is screaming, you are giving it an ability that belongs only to living things. These are examples of personification. Personification is a figure of speech that makes nonliving things act or behave like living things. Personification gives power to objects and allows them to walk, see, speak or imitate human actions.

Examples of Personification

1. My phone has been angry at me since morning.
2. His shoes left him ad stayed back home.
3. Her meal kept calling her to come.
4. The stars wink at us every starry night.
5. The trees danced to the tune of the wind.
6. Lightning ran across the night sky.
7. The hills call us for a feast.
8. The alarm clock on the wall yelled me out of bed.
9. Our car complained as we sped up the hill.

10.   The clouds and the moon are playing hide and seek.

More Examples

1. Her beautiful cap loves her with obvious affection.
2. The staircase groaned as the old lady climbed up.
3. We heard the thunder grumble in the distance
4. I don't know how time flies.
5. The leaves on the ground ran for the lives as the lion chased an antelope.
6. The content of the letter insulted me.
7. My brother's car did not cooperate with him this morning.

8. Onions always make me cry.

9. His hauling truck works very hard for him.

10. The morning newspaper says we should prepare for a storm.

11. My phone died as I was making an important call.

CHAPTER SIX

Synecdoche

Have you ever heard of synecdoche or used it in a sentence before? Synecdoche uses a part of a whole to represent the entire whole. For example, your hand is a part of your body, and synecdoche can use it to represent you as a whole. Your head, leg and arms can stand for the entire body when used in a sentence with synecdoche.

Just like other figures of speech, synecdoche states a fact

by expressing it in a special or an unusual way. Normally, a part of something isn't the entire thing but you're allowed to make it so when using synecdoche.

To construct a good synecdoche, you have to think deeply on what you are about to say. Then look for a part that can fully represent the entire whole. Look at these great examples:

1. I recognized voices in the tunnel.
2. He asked for a hand, and I gave him.
3. I'm going to meet new faces at the party.

4. She needs a shoulder to cry on.
5. Don't disrespect the hand that feed you.
6. I was afraid of the eyes in the large hall.
7. We hired new hands to help in the project.
8. The head count was four million.
9. They drove on two wheels.
10. Those four wheels are not going to last.

More Examples

1. She took her new wheels out for a ride.
2. The government announced that boots are already on the ground.
3. All fingers can't be equal.

4. We lost the best brains to emigration.
5. Take that face away from here.
6. The river doesn't carry off the feet it doesn't see.
7. He hopes to see the pearly gates when he's no more.
8. He was chased down the street by wild whiskers.
9. That blonde hair will make you lose your job.
10. They took the sails and ran off.
11. We get our daily bread through hard work.
12. She rules his heart.

CHAPTER SEVEN

Pun

This figure of speech is suitable for people who like to play with words and make funny jokes. Pun uses words to make things sound humorous, interesting and entertaining. It is the most captivating of all the figures of speech you can use.

Sometimes when a pun is made, it has more than one meaning. But in the end, it makes one to laugh and admire the brilliant play on words. See some examples:

My bicycle is two-tired to stand.

I bought two peanuts that were a-salted.

1. Don't sunbath and read or you become well-red.
2. Push an envelope and it remains stationery.
3. The days on a calendar are all numbered.
4. A dog was arrested for littering.
5. If you touch glue, it will stick to its word.
6. You're mean for calling my teacher average.
7. You don't throw bananas during guerilla warfare.
8. You slip when you sleep.

More Examples

1. With painful soles, I led souls astray.
2. Since I can't read your mind, I can't tell your state.
3. Eating a clock is time-consuming.
4. I was all right after I broke my left arm.
5. I lost interest in my bank.
6. I assisted Santa as one of his subordinate clauses.
7. Grammar taught me comma sense.
8. My lightening was not caused by lightning.
9. The wedding was an emotional one, so the cake came in tiers.
10. When I returned the book to the library, I became shelfish.

CHAPTER EIGHT

Metonymy

Some things can be represented by objects associated with them. These objects are so close to these things that when you see them, you remember the real things they represent. An object like a crown is associated with a king or kingship.

Metonym is a figure of speech that uses a name to represent another with which it is closely related. Just as in our example of crown and kingship, metonymy expresses itself through association of two related objects or ideas.

Look at the following examples:

1. We must respect the crown.
2. Man can end wars though the power of the **pen**.
3. **Swords** are not always effective in times of war.
4. The **White House** issued a statement earlier this morning.
5. She gave me a **dish**.
6. **Hollywood** is the dream of many young actors.
7. We don't understand his **tongue**.
8. No **tongue** can tell what said.

9. Freedom of the **press** is important.

10. **Pentagon** will respond with full force.

More Examples

1. He lent me his **ears** throughout the discussion.
2. She gave me her **hand** when I needed it.
3. It's difficult to find good **heads** these days.
4. **Wise hearts** are scarce to find.
5. **Suits** are getting richer these days.
6. The protesters failed to seize the **throne**.
7. The poor man has four **mouths** to feed at home.
8. I like reading **Shakespeare**.

9. I get help a lot from the
library.

CHAPTER NINE

Euphemism

Good news is pleasant but bad news isn't. We like to talk about positive things but when they are negative, we don't want to talk about them. Even when we do, it gives us great pains to tell others about it. A bad news is when someone loses a job or a loved one. Telling others about what happened is sometimes difficult.

This is where euphemism comes in. Euphemism uses polite and less harsh words to say things that are supposed to sound harsh and unbearable. For instance, instead of saying someone died, you may say the person kicked the bucket or passed away.

Some ways to talk about the death of a loved one:

He is no longer with us.

That uncle is late.

They are deceased.

She has gone home.

That girl has departed here.

Examples of Euphemism

1. He has gone beyond the rainbow. (Died)
2. They resigned their commission. (Sacked)
3. The old man is thin on the top. (Has little hair)
4. She recycled Shakespeare's book. (Plagiarized)
5. Stop being economical with the truth. (Liar)
6. The sick man didn't make it. (Died)
7. He is differently abled. (Disabled)
8. His boss thought of letting him go. (Sacking him)
9. Peter has totally lost his marble. (Mad)
10. She's been knocked up for six months now. (Pregnant)

More Examples

1. She's a girl of easy virtue. (Prostitute)
2. His friend kicked the bucket. (Died)
3. The young boy is visually challenged. (Blind)
4. She is on the big side. (Fat)
5. Too much of junk food made her a curvy woman. (Overweight)
6. Tom spent two years in a correctional facility due to his bad behavior. (Jailed)
7. No, I'm okay, just a little cold. (Serious flu)
8. She was feeling under the weather this morning. (Unwell)
9. May I use the restroom please? (Toilet)

10.   She's at the time of the   month. (Menstruation)
11. The man got plastered. (Drunk)

CHAPTER TEN
Rhetorical Questions

Have you ever asked a question and did not expect an answer? Yes, sometimes we ask these questions consciously or unconsciously. When we do, no one responds to us even though they heard the question we asked. This kind of question is referred to as rhetorical question.

A rhetorical question is a figure of speech that uses a question to make a point instead of waiting for an answer. The aim of a rhetorical question is to make the listener or reader to think deeply about an idea or point. Sometimes, a rhetorical question is used to make people agree to the point the speaker is making.

Examples of Rhetorical Question

1. How Catholic is the Pope?
2. How hot is hell?
3. Do cows moo?
4. Do birds fly?
5. What have I done?
6. Are you for real?
7. Who is to blame?
8. What should I say?
9. Why is this happening to me?
10. What is there to say?

More Examples

1. What's there to talk about?
2. How better can it get?
3. Are you okay?
4. Why do we live to die?
5. What more could we expect?
6. Are you kidding me?
7. Is two and two four?
8. Can you imagine that?
9. Who knows tomorrow?
10. Do we have any other choice?

CHAPTER ELEVEN

Hyperbole

In some situations, we would like to make people to understand how serious or important something is to us. Hyperbole is the figure of speech that helps us to achieve that. For instance, how do you tell someone that you are feeling very hungry or thirsty? How do you show them how tall you or someone else is? How do you help their minds to picture how serious or important something is?

Hyperbole is a figure of speech that exaggerates things in order to make a point. The aim of hyperbole is to help the reader or listener clearly see and understand things.

Examples of Hyperbole

1. This show is taking forever.
2. She cleaned her room a million times.
3. Curtis had a ton of work to do.
4. I'll die if I don't buy a new computer.
5. He walked hundred miles to school in his younger days.
6. My car is faster than lightning.
7. He empties his account to buy that car.

8. My brother was so hungry that he could eat an elephant.
9. She loves me to the moon and back.
10. That animal is dying of thirst.

More Examples

1. I love you more than life itself.
2. This room is killing me with cold.
3. She's addicted to her mobile phone.
4. The princess is more beautiful than the sun.
5. Those workers are so tired that they could sleep for a month.
6. I was so scared that my heart jumped out.

7. I'm dying of hunger right now.

CHAPTER TWELVE

Alliteration

Alliteration is a figure of speech in which words in the same sentence begins with the same consonant sound. Remember that sounds and letters of the alphabet are not the same things. A letter can change its sound when you pronounce it. For example, cell and cake. Cell sounds like the letter **s** while cake sounds like the letter **k.** This is why we say in alliteration the beginning of those words must have the same sounds, not letters.

Examples of Alliteration

1. Curtis called the caregiver.
2. The big black bear bore two babies.
3. Look and learn the little you can.
4. Don't daint the door.
5. Go and get a girl who can gather the goats.
6. She put away her plate, pan and piano.
7. I hurried home to hear him.
8. Ruth remembered her role in the red room.
9. The big boy bounced like a ball.
10. The baker baked beautiful black bread.

More Examples

1. Barry bought bananas and beans.
2. Peter picked peas and peppers properly.
3. The grey gorilla got to the green grass.
4. Bring back the book before my birthday.
5. The snake sneezed and slid on the slide.
6. Paul prayed to partake in paradise.
7. Fred found a funny friend last Friday.
8. Harry heard about the hot hills.
9. Candies killed his cute cat.
10. Bruce broke the bartender's bottles.
11. I gladly gave him good glasses.

CHAPTER THIRTEEN

Antithesis

Almost everything has its opposite or the other side of the same kind of thing. If there's a good idea, there's also a bad idea. Take for an example of a meeting; you stand up and make a new suggestion. Someone else rises up to say something in direct opposition to what you say. This is an example of antithesis.

Antithesis is a figure of speech that places side by side two opposing statements. It is different from oxymoron because oxymoron has to do with two **opposite words** while antithesis is about two **opposite statements**.

Examples of Antithesis

1. Pride leads to demotion; humility leads to exaltation.
2. Humans propose; God disposes.
3. Love is imaginary; marriage is practical.
4. Believe in the best; get ready for the worst.
5. Open your eyes; close your mouth.
6. Give everyone your ear; give a few your voice.
7. Bring friends close; bring your foes closer.
8. Money breeds evil; goodness brings poverty.

9. Be slow in making a choice; be slower in making a change.
10. Spicy food is wow in the mouth but ouch in the tummy.

More Examples

1. No labor, no favor.
2. Skin color matters little; character color matters most.
3. No battle, no victory.
4. Failing to plan is planning to fail.
5. Reigning in hell is better than serving in heaven.
6. You either make or mar your life.
7. Patience is bitter but its fruit is sweet.

8. Know everything about something and something about everything.
9. To stay cool you must burn a fire.
10. Being too slow or too fast makes you miss opportunities.

CHAPTER FOURTEEN

Onomatopoeia

When you read books, you come across words that represent the sounds people or animals make. This is where onomatopoeia comes in. Onomatopoeia is a figure of speech that uses words to represent the sounds around us. In other words, onomatopoeia finds the right word for every sound made by humans, animals and everyday objects.

Onomatopoeia can be either a verb or a noun. For example,

the words 'slap' and 'clap' are both nouns and verbs. Their meanings are clearer when you use them in sentences.

She **slapped** him on the cheek.

That was a **slap** on my reputation.

There was a **clap** of thunder over the sky.

Clap your hands.

Common Onomatopoeic Sounds

Water Sounds

Squirt	Drip
Dribble	Spray
Sprinkle	Splash

Drizzle   Bloop

Object Sounds

Clap   Ding

Bang   Crash

Clatter   Thump

Clang   Clink

Slap   Click

Thud   Bam

Screech   Knock

Crunch   Jingle

Animal Sounds

Bray   Bark

Buzz   Arf

Cluck   Cuckoo

Hiss

Chirp

Cheep

Warble

Tweet

Howl

Purr

Ribbit

Chortle

Cock-a-doodle-doo

Air Sound

Swish

Fwoosh

Waft

Flutter

Fisst

Whip

Whizz

Gasp

Whiff

Swish

Whiff

Human Sounds

Ahem	Blurt
Groan	Chatter
Growl	Eek
Giggle	Murmur
Belch	Mumble
Grunt	Whimper
Gurgle	Squeal
Gulp	Moan

Onomatopoeia in Sentences

1. As the clock made a tick-tock sound, I rose from bed.

2. The village often wakes up at the cock-a-doodle-doo of the village cock.
3. With a click of the mouse, I logged into the website.
4. The children ran away at the moo of the cow.
5. Zip, and was done with zipping my trouser.
6. We couldn't hear what the man said because of the tweets of birds.
7. Buzz buzz, and I suddenly realized that there's a bee hive close by.
8. My teeth chattered after taking a cold shower.
9. Yuk! That was a nasty smell.
10. The sheep baas every time.

More Examples

1. We ran for safety when we heard the terrifying boom outside the window.
2. I like the crunchy sound I make whenever I eat biscuits.
3. Poof! The magician made the hare to appear.
4. The meat deliciously sizzled on the fire.
5. The tires screeched as the car came to a sudden halt.
6. Water drizzled until it drenched our clothes.
7. A sharp knock on the door woke us up.
8. The manager switched on power on the machine whirred to life.
9. Pitter-patter and the rain started to fall.
10. Many kids fear the hoot of owls.

CHAPTER FIFTEEN

Assonance

Assonance is a figure of speech in which similar vowel sounds appear in the same sentence. These sounds are always close to each other in the sentence they appear. For example, the **boy** lost a **toy** in the s**oil**. In the sentence boy, toy and soil have similar vowel sound.

Examples of Assonance

1. He told me to hold on.
2. Let's let the cat out of the bag.

3. He will try and cry for help.
4. Wait and get a mate.
5. He wore a gown and fell down.
6. A stranger is in danger.
7. A crocodile stood a while and made a smile.
8. We ate chicken at eight o clock.
9. Stay focused by keeping your eyes on the prize.
10. She loves eating lean meat.

More Examples

1. He ate a chip and cut his chin.
2. She calls in the fall.
3. My friends mocked when I climbed the rock.
4. The old man was weary as well as teary.

5. A bright light gave us sight.
6. The beggar begged for eggs.
7. I am Sam from San Francisco.
8. A girl came third in the game.
9. The boys make a lot of noise.
10. Our love made us drink from the same cup.

CHAPTER SIXTEEN

Paradox

A paradox is a statement that first appears to sound untrue, unbelievable or false, but a careful look at it, the meaning becomes clear and the reader or listener agreed with the statement. The purpose of paradox is for listeners and readers to pause a little and think about what they read or hear. In that way, the reader develops a deep understanding of the idea being discussed.

Example of Common Paradox

1. Less is more
2. Do what you cannot do.
3. The more you give, the more you get.
4. Live in the present for future sake.
5. Louder means lesser.
6. Change is the only constant thing.
7. You earn more when you spend more.
8. It's strange not to be strange.
9. Everyone tells lies.
10. Truth is not so sweet.

More Examples

1. To be kind, you must first be heartless.

2. Good leader are good followers.
3. True love always hurts in a good way.
4. Something bad can bring something good.
5. Winning and losing are similar.
6. To be yourself you have to lose yourself.
7. Marriage makes one out of two people.
8. To find peace, war is inevitable.
9. Every man's weakness is his strength.
10. To be free, you must become a slave.

CHAPTER SEVENTEEN

Irony

Irony is a figure of speech that compares what is expected and what something really is. In other words, one thing is said and another thing is meant. The speaker says something that has a meaning different from what is said.

You probably have heard many ironic statements from family and friends. Most people use irony in jokes without realizing it.

Examples of Irony

1. Our dentist has a bad toothache.
2. My family sent an Easter card to a Muslim family.
3. The renowned marriage counselor is now a divorcée.
4. After winning the national spelling bee, she failed her class spelling test.
5. A raging fire burnt down the fire station.
6. She posted on Twitter on how useless social media has become.
7. The police officer got arrested by thieves for stealing.
8. Our new English teacher has poor writing and grammar.

9. The ambulance accidentally ran over the man it came to carry to the hospital.

10. He ran from the rain and fell into a river.

About the Publisher

Goodman Publishing is a company dedicated to producing books on English Language, General Studies, Teaching Practice, and the development and learning of listening, writing, reading and speaking skills.

With the help of our professional, trained and experienced staff and contributors, we strive to give our readers the best of experiences.

We understand the importance of the English Language and the reality that the world is fast becoming a global village, thanks to technology. We make our books as simple and understandable as possible so that learners of English will find each topic and volume easy to learn and master.

We publish a new book every month.

Goodman Publishing

www.ingramcontent.com/pod-product-compliance
Lightning Source LLC
Chambersburg PA
CBHW051343150726
48000CB00003B/1025